AND THEN THERE WAS *Ed*

Fishing Mishaps Through the Years

RJ JOHNSON

Library of Congress Control Number: 2024922567

ISBN
978-1-964982-83-0 (Paperback)
978-1-964982-84-7 (eBook)
978-1-964982-82-3 (Hardcover)

This book is dedicated to all fishermen, young and old, who have ever ventured out onto the water with high hopes, only to find themselves entangled in the unpredictable nature of the great outdoors. To those who've cast their lines with anticipation, only to reel in a snag, and to those who've faced one mishap after another yet kept coming back for more, knowing that the next cast could bring the story of a lifetime.

May your love for fishing remain steadfast, your spirits unbroken, and your tales, like the waves, endless. Here's to every misadventure that has shaped you, strengthened you, and—above all—made you laugh.

©RJ Johnson

TABLE OF CONTENTS

The purpose of this book is to share the funny, unexpected things that can happen when you're doing what you love—especially fishing. While fishing might seem peaceful, those of us who've spent time on the water know it can quickly turn into a series of hilarious mishaps.

This book captures those moments—broken gear, stuck boats, and everything else that goes wrong when you're just trying to catch a fish. I hope these stories bring a smile to your face, and maybe even remind you of your own fishing misadventures.

After all, fishing isn't just about the catch—it's about the stories you take home. Enjoy!

ACKNOWLEDGEMENTS

First and foremost, I want to thank my brother-in-law and best friend, Edward Moore—better known as Ed. Without him, most of these mishaps wouldn't have been nearly as memorable or, let's face it, as entertaining. Ed, you've been the perfect partner in this comedy of errors we call fishing.

A special thank you to my wife, Linda, who, without fail, would greet us with the same question every time we returned home: "What happened this time?" Your patience, laughter, and never-ending support have been a blessing.

And to my family, who've shared in the many laughs these stories have provided over the years—thank you for always finding humor in the chaos.

As you dive into the pages of *Fishing Mishaps*, I hope the stories within bring a smile to your face and maybe even a good chuckle. This book isn't just a collection of mishaps on the water; it's the story of how two men—brothers-in-law turned best friends—bonded over their shared love of fishing, mishaps and all.

It all began on a cold, rainy night at a fish stew, when two middle-aged men met for the first time. Both of them were cautiously sizing each other up, wondering if they'd get along. Their initial conversation was polite, but reserved, as if they were both trying to figure out if they could be more than just cordial in-laws. Little did they know, that night was the beginning of a friendship that would weather not just years but countless fishing trips filled with unexpected (and often hilarious) twists and turns.

These "fishing mishaps" are recounted by Randy Johnson with humor and heart, reminding us all that sometimes the best stories come from the moments when things don't go as planned. Each tale is true, and I've heard them all many times, laughing right along with Randy and Ed as they relive their misadventures.

Every time they head off to the coast, my parting words are always, "Be careful, and I love you both." And without fail, the first words out of my mouth when they return are, "What happened this time?"

So, sit back, enjoy these stories, and maybe you'll be reminded of your own fishing mishaps along the way. Here's to good laughs, great memories, and the love of fishing!

Enjoy reading—and happy fishing!

©Linda Johnson (Wife of Randy and Sister to Ed)

This book is a tribute to the joys and chaos of fishing—the moments when everything goes wrong, yet we keep coming back for more. It's about the stubborn hope that drives every fisherman, no matter how many mishaps or disasters strike, to keep casting that line in search of the one that got away. Through all the mishaps, tangled lines, blown tires, and sandbars, there's always the love of the adventure that keeps us going.

I hope these stories not only bring a smile to your face but remind you of the humor and heart that make fishing so unforgettable.

THE FISH STEW SHOWDOWN: MEETING ED

It all started back in 1995 when I was invited to my girlfriend Linda's house for some good old-fashioned fish stew. It was supposed to be a simple evening, but it turned into a night that would change my life in ways I never expected. That evening, I was set to meet her entire family for the first time—a daunting prospect for any new boyfriend. There was her mother, Miss Ella, who I would later affectionately call "Ma," Robert, her youngest brother, Kenneth, her twin brother, and then… there was Ed. Ed, the oldest brother, was the one person I instinctively knew I didn't want to be around.

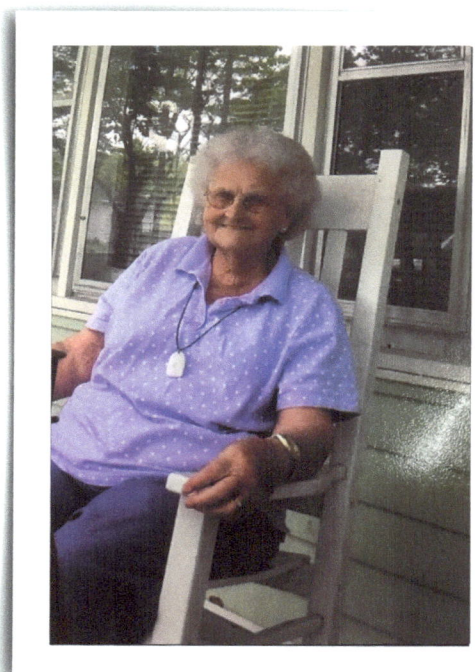

The fish stew was incredible, just as Linda had promised. The evening itself went smoothly, and I found myself enjoying the warmth and banter of her family. Everyone was kind, welcoming, and easy to talk to—everyone except Ed. I couldn't shake the feeling of his eyes on me, scrutinizing every move I made as if he were evaluating me in some secret, brotherly test. Ed's gaze was intense, and though I tried to ignore it, it was impossible not to notice how he kept looking me up and down, as if sizing me up for something.

Despite this, I bonded with Linda's family that night. We laughed, shared stories, and I felt like I was starting to fit in—except for one glaring exception. And then there was Ed. I didn't tell Linda how uncomfortable her older brother made me feel. The last thing

I wanted was to hurt her feelings or make things awkward. So, I kept it to myself, hoping that maybe he'd come around eventually.

As time passed, I got the itch to buy a boat. I wasn't picky—saltwater, freshwater, it didn't matter to me. I just wanted to feel the thrill of being out on the water, casting a line, and maybe even bringing home a good catch. After much deliberation and more than a few trips to various boat dealerships, I finally settled on a 16-foot Lowe boat with a 25-horsepower Johnson motor. It was perfect. There was just one problem—I didn't have anyone to go fishing with.

Linda was terrified of the water, so she was out. Robert had his own boat and usually fished with his son, and Kenneth didn't have any interest in fishing at all.

That left one person. And then there was Ed.

Linda, ever the optimist, suggested I ask Ed to join me. The idea sent a chill down my spine. The thought of being in a confined space, miles from shore, with a man who clearly didn't like me was, to say the least, unsettling. My mind filled with wild thoughts of Ed tossing me overboard with cement blocks tied to my feet. But after a lot of internal debate and a hefty dose of reluctance, I decided to ask him.

Part of me hoped—prayed, really—that he'd say no. But to my utter surprise, Ed didn't just agree; he actually seemed excited about the idea. "I'd love to," he said with a grin that I couldn't quite decipher. And that was how our fishing misadventures began.

Little did I know, those trips would turn into a series of unforgettable—and often hilarious—mishaps that would forever change the way I saw Ed. It turns out that fishing, like life, has a way of bringing people together in the most unexpected ways. And then there was Ed...

THE FIRST MISHAP: THE BEAR AND THE BREAM: A WILD FIRST CATCH

Well, I wasn't entirely sure what to expect, but I was ready to dive into the unknown. So, off we went to New Bern, North Carolina, to a quaint little spot called Brice's Creek. We launched the boat at the ramp and set off with what I hoped would be a peaceful day of fishing.

Right away, I noticed something peculiar: Ed was sporting a sidearm on his hip. "Why are you bringing a gun?" I asked, half-joking, half-worried. Ed just gave me a sly grin and a snicker, leaving me to wonder if I'd inadvertently signed up for some sort of wild adventure. Little did I know, he was simply enjoying the moment, and the best was yet to come.

The first mishap came sooner than I anticipated. We'd found a fantastic spot teeming with bream, crappie, and bass. The fish were practically jumping into the boat, and we managed to bag a decent haul. Feeling pretty proud of ourselves, we decided it was time to head back to the boat ramp.

That's when we encountered our uninvited guest: a massive black bear was lounging right at the ramp. This wasn't just any bear—it was the sort of bear you'd see in wildlife documentaries, the kind that makes you question your life choices. Every time we approached the ramp, the bear would start hopping up and down, like it was challenging us to a duel.

There was no way I was steering that boat toward the ramp with our furry antagonist waiting. We couldn't stay there all day, so I hatched a plan. "Ed, toss one of the fish to the bear," I suggested, hoping to buy us some time.

And then there was Ed, with a mischievous glint in his eye, complied. He flung a fish towards the bear, who caught it mid-air with a swipe of his paw. The bear seemed to contemplate this new offering for a moment, then ambled away, clearly satisfied.

With the ramp finally clear, we managed to dock the boat without further incident. As we unloaded, I couldn't help but laugh at the absurdity of it all. Fishing with Ed turned out to be a series of unpredictable adventures, and I'd learned that sometimes, the best way to deal with life's surprises is to face them head-on—with a little help from your unexpected allies. And as for Ed, well, he was now officially my fishing partner in crime.

And then there was Ed, who tossed the first fish onto the bank, the bear eagerly pounced on it. But, to my dismay, the bear didn't just grab a bite and leave—oh no. He decided to stick around, like he'd just discovered an all-you-can-eat buffet. I told Ed to throw another fish, and again, the bear dutifully chomped it down. This continued until our entire catch had vanished into the bear's voracious appetite.

By the time the bear had stuffed himself silly and finally wandered off, all our fish were gone, and we were left with nothing but the memory of our ill-fated attempt at bear diplomacy. Our day of fishing had turned into a feeding frenzy for a bear with an insatiable appetite.

THE SECOND MISHAP: CLOSE CALLS AND COWLING CHAOS: THE SALTWATER SAGA

With our fish supply depleted, we decided to try our luck in saltwater, thinking a change of scenery might be just what we needed. We packed up and headed to Virginia, where we launched the boat at a local ramp. The first thing I noticed was that with me at the back of the boat and the motor running, water started creeping over the stern. It appeared that my weight, combined with the motor, was a bit too much for our little vessel. We swapped places, and Ed took over the wheel.

As if the day weren't already challenging enough, we had to start bailing water out of the boat. But that was only the beginning. While we were in the middle of the James River, the motor abruptly conked out. We frantically removed the cowling to check the engine, only to discover we were drifting toward the James River bridge—specifically, one of its massive pylons.

There we were, stuck in the current, trying to fix the motor while the boat was slowly, inexorably being drawn toward a very large and immovable object. It was the kind of situation where you can't help but laugh or cry, and I chose to laugh—mostly because I wasn't entirely sure whether we were going to end up as a footnote in the local news.

In our frantic attempt to diagnose the motor's malfunction, we somehow managed to slap the cowling back on upside down. Naturally, it wouldn't fit, which only added to our mounting chaos. Just as we were about to collide with the pylon, the motor roared to life, and we shot off into the river, narrowly avoiding disaster.

Miraculously, the rest of the day turned out quite enjoyable. The fishing was decent, and, thankfully, Ed had left his sidearm at home, which was a huge relief to me. Over time, we'd gone from awkward acquaintances to genuine friends—brothers-in-law who had weathered their share of mishaps together. But our adventures weren't over yet.

While fishing, we drifted close to the Newport shipyard, a facility known for its naval repairs. It seemed we'd ventured a bit too near, because soon enough, two gunboats emerged from the shipyard, their guns trained on us in a show of maritime authority. It didn't take us long to figure out we'd crossed an invisible line.

We quickly learned the hard way that there are rules about how close you can get to a shipyard. But hey, it's not every day you get to experience a naval standoff firsthand. By the end of the day, we had plenty of stories to laugh about and an invaluable lesson in maritime etiquette.

We attempted to start the motor again, but, of course, it refused to cooperate. And where were we drifting? Right back toward the shipyard! To say we were terrified of becoming target practice for the naval guns would be an understatement. The shipyard's guns were far from friendly, and we had no intention of finding out just how precise they were. Finally, with a sputter and a roar, the motor miraculously started, and we made a beeline back to the boat ramp. We loaded up and hightailed it out of there.

THE THIRD MISHAP: RAMP RAGE: CROAKERS AND CHAOS AT THE DOCK

Our next fishing trip took us back to Virginia, driven by a craving for the famed big croakers of James River. We launched the boat at the ramp, careful to avoid the shipyard this time. We navigated safely, caught a cooler full of those tasty croakers, and were feeling pretty triumphant.

But the day's peace was about to be shattered. As the afternoon wore on, I found myself behind the wheel as we headed back to the ramp. My mind, apparently vacationing on Mars, led me to bypass the waiting fleet of about seven or eight boats and pull directly into the ramp. Not my finest moment!

As I hopped out to fetch the truck and back the trailer into the water, a scene straight out of a sitcom unfolded. A rather indignant lady—let's just say she had a robust presence—started laying into Ed. She was practically fuming and declared she'd call the Marine police if she could. And, truth be told, she had every right to be upset.

Instead of a polite apology, Ed decided to up the ante. He shot back at her, "Go ahead, call the blankety-blank police!" My jaw dropped as I realized that Ed, in all his wisdom, was ready to pick a fight with a decidedly non-threatening lady. There we were, in a state where we knew no one, and Ed was ready to go toe-to-toe with a local who was clearly more bark than bite.

I quickly suggested we haul the boat up a bit further and tie it down. As I did, the verbal exchange continued, with Ed seemingly determined to escalate things. Meanwhile, I couldn't help but think how this day had gone from fishing success to a comedy of errors, and all we needed now was to make a hasty exit before things got any more absurd.

I couldn't help but notice the lady's husband, who looked like he might weigh all of 100 pounds soaking wet, shaking his head with an expression that screamed, "I hope I'm not in for a fight today." Finally, I managed to wrangle Ed into the truck, and we sped away, escaping the scene.

THE FOURTH MISHAP: LOST AT SEA: NAVIGATING WAVES, WAKES, AND THE COAST GUARD

Our next fishing adventure took us to our own coast in Eastern North Carolina, between Morehead City and Beaufort. By now, we were starting to learn the ropes of boating—albeit the hard way. We launched our boat at a pleasant ramp across from Radio Island.

We set off with high spirits, navigating around the bridge towards the ocean from the port. As we approached Fort Macon, we were blissfully unaware of how the water conditions would change.

Before long, we found ourselves surrounded by waves that looked about seven or eight feet high. It felt like we were in a scene from a disaster movie, locked in a 16-foot boat built for creek fishing.

Panic set in as I told Ed to get us out of there, but the boat motor, predictably, refused to start. We were drifting further into the ocean, and our tiny vessel seemed increasingly out of place among the towering waves. Eventually, the motor roared back to life, and we made a hasty escape.

We managed to catch some fish at the port, which was a relief, and headed back to the ramp. However, our luck ran out again when we were flagged down by the Coast Guard. Apparently, our little boat was creating a wake in a no-wake zone. The Coast Guard, not exactly known for their tact, sternly instructed us to slow down. I felt a strange sense of pride that our modest boat was causing enough of a splash to warrant attention from the big guys. We kept our latest experiences in mind, hoping to avoid future blunders.

THE FIFTH MISHAP: A HITCH TOO FAR: THE BOAT THAT NEARLY BLEW UP

Considering our Virginia escapades, we decided it was best to lay low for a while and return to familiar waters in Morehead City and Beaufort. By this time, I had upgraded to a used boat with a 200 hp Mercury motor, believing I'd struck gold with this purchase. We were thrilled to have a bigger boat—a 22-foot Wellcraft with a T-top.

Our first outing with the new boat was supposed to be a thrilling adventure, but fate had other plans. As we drove through New

Bern on our way to Morehead City, the unthinkable happened—the boat and trailer detached from the truck hitch. And, as if the universe had a twisted sense of humor, the boat started rolling toward some gas tanks at a nearby gas station!

Panic surged through me as I imagined the boat crashing into those gas pumps and triggering the biggest explosion since the Big Bang. In a heart-pounding maneuver, I managed to steer the runaway trailer away from the gas tanks, narrowly avoiding a catastrophe. We ended up coming to a stop right next to them, our hearts racing and nerves on edge.

Neither Ed nor I could budge the boat trailer with the boat still on it, and securing it back onto the hitch seemed like a Herculean task. Just as despair was starting to set in, three good Samaritans appeared on the scene. They looked like they might have been Marines from Cherry Point Air Base in Havelock, but honestly, I was too relieved to care.

With a combined effort that seemed almost choreographed, these heroes lifted the trailer back onto the hitch, securing it with impressive efficiency. Their timely intervention saved the day, and with a mixture of gratitude and embarrassment, we continued on our way, our adventure now enriched with yet another unforgettable mishap.

THE SIXTH MISHAP: WAKE-UP CALL: THE MARINE POLICE SHOWDOWN

After our harrowing experience with the boat trailer and those gas pumps, we finally made it to Morehead City and Beaufort. We launched the boat at our usual spot and set off, eager to escape the day's earlier chaos. But as soon as we cleared the bridge and hit open water, Ed, in his infinite wisdom, decided to floor it. It was like watching a man possessed by the spirit of speed.

Ed was practically a lunatic behind the wheel, and it felt like we were in a high-speed chase rather than a leisurely fishing trip. It seemed he'd forgotten our previous run-in with the law. No sooner had we picked up speed than we heard the blaring siren and saw flashing blue lights in our rearview. It was the Marine police, and boy, was the officer a stickler for rules.

This guy was the epitome of no-nonsense, and he wasted no time laying down the law. He wrote Ed up for speeding through a no-wake zone and made it crystal clear that our names were now on the radar. If we got caught again, the fine would be steep. At that moment, Ed's understanding of what a no-wake zone meant was suddenly and painfully clear.

Despite our nerves being frazzled and our egos bruised, we slowed our pace and carried on with the fishing trip. Remarkably, we managed to have a successful day on the water, catching plenty of fish. It was a classic case of a day that started with a series of unfortunate events but ended with some satisfaction, even if the journey there was a rollercoaster of its own.

THE SEVENTH MISHAP: BAITED AND SWITCHED: THE DAY ED GOT HOOKED

When we rolled up to the boat ramp, our eyes fell upon an attractive lady in a miniskirt, with a figure that could still turn heads—even at our age. Sure, we might be in our seventies, but a little harmless admiration never hurt anyone. As I hopped out of the boat and started backing the truck into the water, I noticed Ed was deep in conversation with the lady. She had made her way right up the dock where Ed was, leaving me to wonder what was going on.

As I maneuvered the truck and boat into position, the lady breezed by me without even a glance or a "hello." Once we got the boat on the trailer and pulled up to secure it, Ed was grinning from ear to ear, his bearded face looking like the cat that caught the canary. "Well, the ole boy's still got it!" he declared.

Confused, I asked him what he was talking about. Ed proudly informed me that the stunning woman had approached him and offered to clean his boat. I had to break the news to him that this 'beautiful lady' was actually a police officer posing as a hooker. If Ed had handed over any cash, he'd have been in a world of trouble, and I'd be heading home solo.

I'd noticed a couple of guys in a vehicle parked in the law enforcement spot marked by a sign, which clued me in. And let's be honest—I knew I was way better looking than Ed, and she hadn't given me a second glance!

Ed's face dropped like a deflated balloon as he realized he'd been duped. For once, I had the chance to laugh my butt off at Ed, instead of him getting the last laugh. To this day, we refer to that place as "THE PLACE OF THE EVENT"—a private joke between us, until now.

THE EIGHT MISHAP: ED'S EMERGENCY EXIT: THE STOMACH VIRUS SHOWDOWN

This time, we headed back to Virginia, and let me tell you, it was a disaster from the start! Ed had been battling a stomach virus, but in typical Ed fashion, he insisted we go fishing anyway. So, off we went. After checking into the trusty Econo Lodge in Carrollton, I took one look at Ed—he was pale as a ghost. "You sure you wanna do this?" I asked. "Yep," he grumbled. Bad decision, Ed. Bad decision.

We launched the boat and headed straight to our favorite fishing spot. I was up at the front, happily casting my line, when suddenly, I heard a sound that was, quite frankly, alarming. It wasn't the motor cranking. I spun around and—there it was—Ed, pants around his ankles, butt hanging off the back of the boat, doing what can only be described as a public display of gastrointestinal distress. And I mean *right there*—in front of God, the fish, and any poor souls who happened to be nearby!

Now, I've seen a lot in my years of fishing, but nothing quite like that. I reeled my line in so fast you'd think I was fighting a record-breaking marlin. There was no way I was catching anything in that part of the river after Ed had… well, christened it.

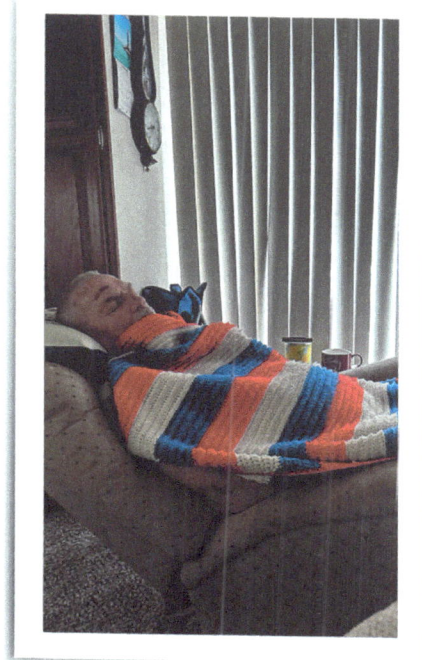

When he finally pulled himself together, I didn't waste a second. We headed straight back to the motel. Ed collapsed onto the bed and stayed there like a sack of potatoes until 2 PM the next day. When he finally crawled out of bed, I didn't even ask if he was up for more fishing. We packed up and high-tailed it home.

That trip is forever burned into my memory as the day Ed's stomach called the shots—and not in a good way. I'll never forget it for as long as I live!

THE NINTH MISHAP: WHEN GOOD INTENTIONS MEET MECHANICAL MAYHEM

It was supposed to be a simple fishing trip—just like the nine other "simple" fishing trips before it. This time, we headed back to Virginia, eager for a weekend filled with sun, water, and a cooler packed with fresh fish. Ed, as always, was buzzing with excitement, convinced this was going to be *the trip* where everything went smoothly. I, on the other hand, had my doubts. By then, I had learned that "smooth" and "Ed" never quite belonged in the same sentence.

We spent the night in a local motel—a little roadside gem with creaky beds and a sign that flickered "Vacan y" as if the "C" had given up halfway through the job. After tossing and turning all night (thanks to Ed's snoring that could rival a foghorn), we were up at the crack of dawn, bleary-eyed but determined.

The next morning, we made our way to the dock. There she was—the Wellcraft. A beauty of a boat, glistening in the early morning sun, practically begging to hit the water. We unloaded our gear, filled up the cooler with ice, and got everything ready for a day of fishing glory. Ed, of course, had that gleam in his eye—the one that always signaled he was ready to out-fish everyone in sight. I could already hear him gloating about the "big one" he was bound to catch.

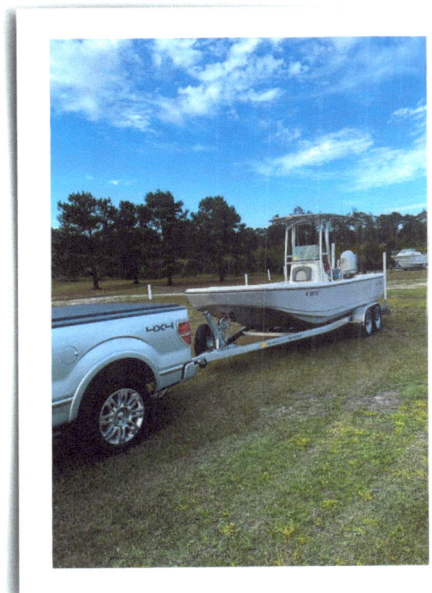

But then, just as we were about to launch, disaster struck. Again. The motor wouldn't crank. And let me tell you, this wasn't the first time that particular piece of machinery had decided to ruin our plans. I stared at it in disbelief, half-expecting it to start smoking just for dramatic effect. I glanced at Ed, who was already muttering under his breath, his face turning a shade of red that could only mean one thing—choice words were on their way.

And boy, did they come. Ed unleashed a string of curses so colorful I swear the birds flying overhead paused mid-flight just to listen. I stood there, nodding, because what else could I do? Neither Ed nor I were boat mechanics, and truth be told, if you handed us anything more complicated than duct tape and baling wire, we were in over our heads.

But Ed, never one to back down from a challenge, gave it a go anyway. He fiddled with the motor, cursed at it some more, and even gave it a couple of well-aimed kicks. I watched, arms crossed, knowing full well this was going nowhere. But, as always, you can't tell Ed that.

"If this thing could be fixed with baling wire and duct tape, we'd be out there right now pulling in fish by the dozen," I muttered, earning a glare from Ed that suggested I was about five seconds away from being tossed into the water.

After another hour of grumbling, tinkering, and kicking (because apparently, Ed believed physical violence might somehow motivate the motor into working), we admitted defeat. The Wellcraft sat there mocking us as we loaded everything back up. And just like that, our grand fishing expedition was over before it even began.

To add insult to injury, the whole ordeal had cost us around $500 between the motel, food, gas, and, of course, the essential fishing gear Ed had insisted we needed. And what did we have to show for it? No fish, a broken boat, and a long, silent drive back home with Ed gripping the wheel like it owed him money.

As we pulled into the driveway, Ed looked over at me, still seething but with a hint of that stubborn optimism that made him Ed.

"Well," he said finally, "there's always next time."

I didn't have the heart to remind him that next time was just as likely to end with us stuck in another motor fiasco. But, as always, I nodded and smiled. After all, when it comes to fishing trips with Ed, the mishaps are half the fun—even if they cost you an arm and a leg.

THE TENTH MISHAP: BLOWOUTS, BOONDOGGLES, AND ONE-LEGGED HEROES

By the time the fishing trip rolled around, you'd think we would've learned. But no, when it came to fishing misadventures, Ed and I were like moths to a flame—an adventure just waiting to happen. This trip was no different from the rest, except that this time, the disaster struck not on the water but on the way home. We had just finished a decent day of fishing down at Morehead City, packed up the boat, and hit the road, feeling pretty good about ourselves. For once, we thought we might make it through a trip unscathed.

And then, just as we were cruising along, feeling invincible, it happened.

BAM!

In a split second, smoke started billowing out from under the trailer. I glanced in the side mirror and saw one of the trailer tires completely shredded, flapping around like a limp noodle.

"Blown tire," I muttered, already feeling the dread sink in.

Ed's response was a mix of frustration and determination. "We've got two wheels on each side of the trailer. One blowout isn't gonna stop us. We'll just keep going on the three we've got left."

Now, I should've known better than to agree, but sometimes you just go along with Ed's logic because fighting it only leads to more trouble. So, we pressed on, hoping we could make it the rest of the way back to Kinston without another incident.

But of course, this was us—Ed and me—and nothing is ever that easy.

BAM!

Less than a minute later, the second tire on the same side blew out. I watched in disbelief as the trailer sagged to one side, smoke pouring out even faster. We were done for. Two flat tires and one spare. The kind of luck that only seemed to follow us around.

So there we were, stranded on the side of the highway, looking at each other in that familiar "Well, now what?" kind of way. And let me tell you, when it comes to mechanical skills, Ed and I together might be worth 50 cents, and even that's being generous. There was no way we could fix this on our own.

As we sat there, scratching our heads and contemplating our next move, a young guy came jogging by. I figured he might just jog on past us, but to our surprise, he stopped and offered to help. He tried everything—fiddling with the trailer, checking the tires, and giving us advice—but it was hopeless. We were well beyond the point of a quick roadside fix.

Just when I thought the situation couldn't get any more surreal, another good Samaritan pulled over. But this wasn't just any man—this was a one-legged man. Now, I'm all for not judging a book by its cover, but when a guy with one leg shows up to help fix two flat tires, you can't help but wonder if the universe is messing with you.

Bless his heart, he tried. He stood there, barking instructions at the young jogger like a drill sergeant, directing him on what to do with the spare tire. The jogger did his best to follow along, but nothing worked. We were stuck, and no amount of effort from either of them was going to change that.

After what felt like an eternity of trial and error, I finally remembered something important. "Wait a second," I said, smacking my forehead. "I've got insurance on the boat. Trailer repair and towing are included."

Ed just stared at me for a second before letting out a long, exasperated sigh. "You're telling me we've been sitting here all this time, and you've got a way out?"

I grinned sheepishly. "Better late than never, right?"

I called the insurance company, and within about half an hour, a tow truck showed up, much to Ed's relief. The driver loaded the boat onto the back of the truck, and we followed him to the next town—New Bern—where he dropped the boat off in a shopping center parking lot. And not just any parking lot—no, this was the one right next to a Food Lion. There's something about seeing your boat parked next to grocery carts that really drives home just how absurd your life has become.

We headed home that night, defeated but still holding onto a shred of humor. The next day, we came back to New Bern with two new tires, fixed up the trailer, and finally made it back to Kinston without further incident.

As we pulled into the driveway, Ed looked over at me and shook his head. "We can't make it through a single trip without some kind of disaster, can we?"

I chuckled, slapping him on the back. "Well, at least we're consistent."

THE ELEVENTH MISHAP: STRANDED ON SANDBARS AND SAILING THROUGH SURPRISES

Picture this: it was a bright morning, and Ed and I were feeling optimistic for once. We had a camper down at Stella where we liked to stay for a couple of days and get in some solid fishing. This time, the plan was to put the boat in at the Swansboro boat ramp. Everything went smoothly—no hiccups with the trailer, the boat started right up, and we managed to get it in the water without a single problem. Naturally, we started thinking, "Hey, maybe today's the day we finally catch a break."

Yeah, no.

Things were going fine for about, oh, ten minutes, until Ed was driving along, and out of nowhere—**BAM!**—we came to a dead stop.

"Sandbar," Ed muttered, as if just saying the word would magically free us from it.

There we were, smack in the middle of a giant sandbar, stuck fast. No amount of cursing, rocking the boat, or sheer willpower was going to get us out of this one. We were stranded, and no matter how much Ed revved the motor or tried to shove us free with an oar, we didn't budge an inch.

After what felt like hours of sitting there, contemplating whether we'd become permanent fixtures of Swansboro's boating scene, a nice gentleman and his wife pulled up in their boat nearby. The man took one look at our predicament and offered to help. Bless him, he didn't even laugh—at least not openly.

We tied his anchor rope to ours, creating some sort of makeshift towing system, and prayed this would work. The man tried backing his boat, pulling ours at the same time, but nothing. We were stuck harder than we thought.

Then another boater pulled up. And instead of offering to help, what did this guy do? He took a picture. That's right—our embarrassing misfortune was now immortalized in some stranger's vacation photo album.

He did, however, suggest something useful after getting his snapshot. "Why don't you untie the anchor rope, turn your boat around, and try pulling them out forward instead of backward?"

It was so simple it just might work.

So, we got everything set up. I was on one side of our boat, and Ed was on the other, both of us ready to jump in the second our boat got unstuck. The man in the other boat tightened up the line, hit the throttle, and took off with everything he had.

And when I say our boat *moved*, I mean it shot off that sandbar like a bat out of hell. One second, it was stuck solid, and the next, it was gliding over the water like it had never been stuck at all.

Now here's the part that still makes me laugh to this day: I didn't get in the boat. I tried, but the thing took off so fast I was left standing there on the sandbar, ankle-deep in water, looking like a complete idiot.

But Ed? Oh, Ed made it into the boat, and I swear I've never seen an old man move so fast in my life. One second, he was right beside me, and the next, he was in the boat, waving and thanking the guy who had helped us like nothing had happened. He was just standing there, chit-chatting away, while I stood on the sandbar, abandoned, looking like some kind of tourist attraction.

And then it started: boaters passing by slowed down, not to offer help, but to **wave**. I felt like I was in a parade, standing in the middle of the water, as boat after boat cruised past, their passengers giving me cheerful waves and thumbs-up as if this whole scene was some kind of entertainment for them. I half expected someone to start selling popcorn.

Finally, after what felt like an eternity of waving back at my "adoring fans," I managed to get Ed's attention.

"Hey, you planning on leaving me here or what?"

Ed looked back, saw me standing there, and with a grin, he swung the boat around and pulled up close enough for me to hop in.

I plopped down in the boat, soaked and salty in more ways than one. "To heck with fishing," I muttered.

Just as we were about to head back to the camper, something magical happened. A flash of pink in the distance caught our eyes. I sat up, squinting to see what it was. Ed looked too, and before we could even say a word, up from the water rose the most beautiful, rare sight: a pink dolphin. It arched gracefully through the waves, catching the sunlight in a way that made it shimmer like some kind of otherworldly creature. For a moment, we both forgot about the sandbar, the frustration, even the boat parade. It was like a little gift from the ocean, as if to say, "You may have had a rough day, but here's something to make it all worth it."

The dolphin disappeared back into the water, leaving us both sitting there, stunned into silence. We may not have caught any fish that day, but we caught a glimpse of something much rarer—a sight that made all the mishaps seem a little less significant.

With a new sense of wonder, we headed back to the camper. No fish, no trophy catch, but we had a story to tell. And isn't that what fishing's all about?

THE TWELFTH MISHAP: DEAD MOTORS AND REPEATED RESCUES

This one's actually a two-for-one deal—two mishaps rolled into one because, well, when you're Ed and me, that's just how it goes.

Now, if you've spent any time around these parts, especially if you own a boat and fancy yourself a fisherman in the open ocean, there are a couple of things that are pretty much written in stone. First, you absolutely, without question, better have a marine radio. And second, you must, should, and really ought to have a membership with SeaTow or one of those other rescue services. These are the folks who come to your rescue when things inevitably go sideways out there on the water. Because trust me, sooner or later, they will.

So, let's set the scene: your miles offshore, enjoying a peaceful day, and then—out of nowhere—your motor gives up on life. You're dead in the water. Now what? You can't exactly call AAA to come tow you back to shore. But, if you've got a marine radio—and if you're smart, you've also got SeaTow—you can radio for help. And don't forget, you'll need a solid GPS on your boat. Why? Because when you make that call, the first thing they're going to ask you is, "What's your location?"

Now, I'm telling you this because Ed and I have found ourselves in not one, but two, such situations. Yes, twice! Imagine that.

The first time, we were out there, just cruising along, thinking we had everything under control (a dangerous thought when you're with Ed, by the way), and **boom**—the motor cuts out like a light. No warning, no sputter, just dead. Of course, we had no idea what was wrong, and even if we did, it's not like either of us could fix it. Neither one of us is exactly what you'd call "mechanically inclined." Heck, between the two of us, we couldn't fix a broken shoelace, let alone a boat engine.

But, luckily for us, we had the radio. And Ed, who at least knows how to operate that thing, gets on and radios for help. "SeaTow, this is *your new best friends*. We're stuck out here off the coast, and we need a tow."

Now, here's where the GPS comes in. The first thing the guy on the other end asks is, "What's your location?"

I looked at Ed, Ed looked at me, and we both looked down at the GPS—thankfully, we had one. There it was, flashing our coordinates like a beacon of hope. We relayed the numbers, and after what felt like an eternity of waiting, there came the glorious sight of SeaTow's yellow boat on the horizon, like a knight in shining armor.

The second time? Well, wouldn't you know it, we found ourselves in the same situation—different day, same result. There we were, drifting along, and **thunk**—the engine quit again. By this point, we were practically experts at calling for a tow. Ed was back on the radio in a heartbeat. "Hey, it's us again… yep, same problem. Yep, we're in the same general area. Yep, we've got the GPS coordinates ready for you."

I could hear the guy chuckle on the other end. "You boys again? You really oughta think about switching mechanics."

So, here's my free advice to every fisherman with a boat who plans on venturing into the ocean: make sure you've got a marine radio, a membership with SeaTow, and a good GPS. Trust me, when that motor gives out, and your miles from shore, you'll thank me.

Because if you're anything like Ed and me, the only thing you'll be catching that day is a ride back to the dock.

THE THIRTEENTH MISHAP: LOCKED TIRES AND LOWE'S LIFESAVERS

Ah, deja vu! It was just another one of those days when you start to think that fate has a peculiar sense of humor when it comes to us. We were heading from our trusty camper to our favorite fishing spot, spirits high and gear in tow, when—*BAM*! Another tire blew out. You'd think we'd be used to it by now, but each new incident still managed to catch us off guard.

This time, I'd learned a thing or two from our previous mishaps. Instead of limping along and risking more damage, I quickly pulled into a nearby subdivision, hoping for some relief. But, of course, our luck had its own plans. The spare tire was securely mounted on the boat trailer and, to add insult to injury, it was fastened with a chain and a lock. Yes, a lock.

And guess who didn't have the key to the lock? That's right—yours truly.

Enter Ed, stage left. With his usual flair for making things sound simpler than they are, Ed announces, "We're gonna need to cut that chain to get the tire off the trailer." Brilliant idea, Ed! However, as I pointed out, "We don't have a tool for that."

But Ed, being the eternal optimist and self-proclaimed problem-solver, was undeterred. I, on the other hand, was starting to feel the weight of the situation. Thankfully, I remembered there was a Lowe's just a couple of miles away. So, we unhooked the boat and trailer, and I set off with a determined stride towards the store.

At Lowe's, I picked up a set of bolt cutters. After what felt like an eternity of navigating the aisles and waiting in line, I was back at the scene of the mishap. With the new bolt cutters in hand, we jacked up the trailer with the trusty jack I'd brought along, and Ed and I wrestled with the chain. It was a bit of a struggle, but eventually, the chain gave way, and the spare tire was free.

We swapped out the blown tire for the spare, reconnected the boat trailer to the truck, and with a collective sigh of relief, we continued on our journey.

Note to self—and to anyone who might find themselves in a similar predicament: when traveling with a spare tire, make sure it's in the back of the truck, not locked up on the trailer!

And thus ended yet another episode in the ongoing saga of Ed and me, proving once again that while we might not always have the right tools or the best luck, we've certainly mastered the art of improvisation and persistence.

THE FOURTEENTH MISHAP: FENDER BENDERS AND FINANCIAL FIASCOS

This time, our fishing trip in Morehead City had started off promisingly. The day was bright, the fish were biting, and we'd managed to haul in a decent catch. Spirits were high as we made our way back to the boat ramp, eagerly anticipating a smooth end to our outing.

But as we pulled into the parking lot, our mood took a nosedive. To our dismay, we discovered that someone had crashed into our boat trailer. The damage was significant—a fender was nearly torn off, and the tail light on the truck was shattered. The sight was enough to make anyone's blood boil.

Ed, never one to hold back, let loose a string of expletives that would make a sailor blush. Amidst the colorful language, we managed to get the boat back onto the trailer, despite the compromised fender threatening to further complicate the process.

Determined to salvage what was left of our day, we headed home. On the way, I stopped by a repair shop to get an estimate for fixing the damage. To my utter shock, the repair bill came in at around $500! My jaw nearly hit the floor. Fishing had suddenly turned into an expensive hobby, and the cost of repairs was turning out to be a bottomless pit.

As of three months later, the boat is still in the repair shop. The mechanics have been struggling to find a replacement fender that matches, and the saga of the broken trailer fender continues. It seems that our fishing adventures come with more than just tales of the one that got away—they're also packed with unexpected repairs and a hefty price tag.

THE FIFTEENTH AND THE FINAL MISHAP: A ROD, A REEL, AND A LESSON IN LETTING GO

This trip was meant to be a special one. I decided to take my two granddaughters, Summer and Jenna—whom I love dearly—along for a day of fishing. They had been eagerly looking forward to this adventure, and I was excited to share the experience with them.

Before heading out, I had splurged on a brand-new rod and reel, eager to let one of the girls use it. As luck would have it, Summer was the fortunate one chosen to christen the new equipment. We arrived at our favorite fishing spot, and Jenna was already busy with her line in the water, happily casting away.

I focused on teaching Summer how to handle the new rod and reel. With a mix of pride and anticipation, I guided her through the motions. We took a deep breath, drew the rod back, and made a perfect cast. Or so I thought. To my horror, as we followed through, the entire rod and reel—brand new and sparkling—went flying off the end of the line and straight into the ocean.

For a moment, I stood there, stunned and speechless, with tears welling up in my eyes. I struggled to find the right words, knowing how disappointed Summer must have felt. I forced a smile and tried to reassure her, saying, "Don't worry about it; it's just a rod and reel."

Just a rod and reel? In reality, it was a $150 piece of equipment that had vanished into the deep blue. I tried to stay positive for the sake of the girls, but inside, I was a mix of regret and frustration. It was a mishap that would be remembered for years to come, a fishing trip that ended with a splash and a valuable lesson about the unpredictability of the sea.

THE GRAND FINALE MISHAP: MEATBALLS, HOT SAUCE, AND THE ART OF SURVIVING ED'S KITCHEN

At the end of every fishing trip Ed and I embark on, there's a sacred tradition—Ed does the cooking, and I, well, I reap the rewards!

Now, for those of you wondering, yes, Ed handles all the fish cleaning too. I'm more of the "supervisor" in this arrangement. My role? I sit back, maybe offer some moral support, and enjoy the final product. It's a pretty sweet deal if you ask me.

Ed takes pride in his cooking. He's the kind of guy who can fry up fish to golden, crispy perfection, or whip up a hearty stew like it's second nature. But sometimes, even the best chefs have a bit of a "mishap." Take the infamous meatball incident, for instance.

One evening, after a successful (or so we thought) fishing day, Ed decided to make meatballs—something a little different from the usual fried fish. Everything was going fine until he knocked over an entire bottle of Texas Pete hot sauce into the pot.

Now, you'd think maybe he would stop, try to salvage the situation, or at least dilute the disaster. Nope. In typical Ed fashion, he shrugged and said, "Eh, a little heat never hurt anyone." Famous last words.

When those meatballs hit the table, they looked delicious. But one bite in, and I swear I saw my life flash before my eyes. It was like biting into a molten lava ball. My mouth was on fire!

Ed, of course, was chewing away like nothing happened, but I couldn't even speak. I was too busy trying to fan my face and down water like it was going out of style. Finally, Ed caught on—probably because I was turning an alarming shade of red—and admitted they might've been "a bit spicy."

We had to make an emergency trip to the freezer for ice cream, and I'm pretty sure I still felt the burn three days later. But even with the mishap, we had a good laugh about it (once the fire in my mouth subsided).

But I'll tell you this—nothing beats Ed's fried fish. Crispy on the outside, tender on the inside, it's our go-to after a long day of mishaps on the water. Me? I can barely make a sandwich, so I leave the cooking to the expert.

So, at the end of every fishing trip, no matter how chaotic the day has been—whether it's blown tires, lost gear, or sandbars—we can always count on Ed's cooking to wrap things up on a high note. And though there's always a little unpredictability when Ed's in charge of the kitchen (like a surprise dash of too much Texas Pete), that's all part of the adventure.

After all, fishing isn't just about what you catch—it's about the stories, the laughs, and the memories that come with every trip. And, of course, a good meal shared with your best friend.